Happiness is never better exhibited
than by young animals, such as puppies,
kittens, lambs, &c., when playing
together, like our own children.

—**Charles Darwin**

# ELEPHANT BOWLING

## and Other Animal Play

**Richard Haynes**

illustrated by **Stephanie Laberis**

CANDLEWICK PRESS

# CONTENTS

Polar Bear

Wolf

Raven

NORTH AMERICA

Beaver

Columbian Ground Squirrel

North American River Otter

Dolphin

Hare

Green Heron

Hummingbird

Sea Lion

SOUTH AMERICA

Neotropic Cormorant

Cactus Finch

EUROPE

ASIA

Japanese
Macaque

Arabian
Babbler

Mongoose

Rhesus
Monkey

Lowe's Guenon
Monkey

AFRICA

Mountain
Gorilla

Chimpanzee

Orangutan

Kangaroo

Bonobo

Saltwater
Crocodile

AUSTRALIA

Spotted
Hyena

Kea

Meerkat

Seagull

Rainbow Lorikeet

# INTRODUCTION

## Who Wants to Play?

Humans love to play. It feels good and can get us laughing until we're holding our sides. When we get lost in play, our bodies release hormones—such as dopamine, serotonin, oxytocin, cortisol, and adrenaline—brain chemicals that fill us with positive feelings and help our bodies function.

For example, think of running while playing a game of tag. Our muscles work hard to keep us from getting caught. The giggles and fun we have at play release "happy hormones." This helps our bodies feel better, more relaxed, and eager to keep going, which fuels us with energy.

The games we play help our bodies and minds grow and develop. This is important because a time may come when speed and quick wits are needed to outrun a big, barking dog, or even the sting of a mad hornet.

Part I of this book takes a look at animal play that has a purpose. About 80 percent of animals in the wild engage in play for similar reasons: to develop strength and agility as they learn and hone strategies and skills necessary to survive in the wild.

Scientists believe that, like humans, animals need "happy hormones," too. They have observed that when animals feel safe, secure, and healthy, playtime can begin.

A child might invite a friend to play by smiling, holding out a ball, and asking, "Hey, wanna play catch?" But how do animals know when it's playtime? If a kangaroo is looking for a good time, a back-and-forth shake of the head means "Let's play!" A wolf will lower its head and front paws and stick its rump in the air. A chimpanzee puts on its play face, which looks a lot like a human smile. The kea parrot sends out a warbling signal—*ha-ha, ha-ha-ha*—until a parrot party is in full swing. These are but a few of the signals animals use to start the fun.

Part II of this book highlights animal play that is purely for the fun of it. Animals entertain themselves by playing dress-up or hide-and-seek, by blowing bubbles or dancing. It appears that animals, like us, have a sense of humor. They tease, taunt, and try to outwit their playmates. At other times, they toss a found object just to watch and hear it fall.

From elephants that bowl to crocodiles that surf to river otters that juggle to monkeys that play peekaboo, animals the world over love to let the good times roll.

# PART I

# THE OBJECT OF THE GAME

# GAMES OF SPEED AND AGILITY

**Zoom! Zoom! Zoomie!**
Two wolves tear off running at top speed, darting around trees, rocks, dirt mounds, and bushes. Wolves are apex predators and must take down fast and formidable game in order to live. The speed and muscles developed during these madcap races help them to catch and overpower moose and elk.

## Catch Me If You Can

A sea lion grabs a piece of kelp and waves it around to tempt another sea lion into a friendly high-speed chase. If they run out of air before playtime is over, they'll surface, grab a quick gulp of air, then dive back into the game, sometimes holding their breath for as many as eight to twenty minutes. These underwater gymnastics push their muscles to the limit and stretch lung capacity, two things that can help them outswim a hungry orca or fearsome shark.

Beaver pups also spin, somersault, and juke with one another underwater, play that prepares them to dart, dive, and disappear when a hungry otter comes prowling.

Columbian ground squirrels, found in the Pacific Northwest and southwestern Canada, rush at each other to signal the start of a game of chase. These twisting gyrations sharpen their swift reactions to elude a quick-eyed hawk.

Dwarf mongooses, of East and southern Central Africa, likewise spring into the air, turn somersaults, and chase their own tails. This mongoose ballet comes in handy when a deadly snake or jackal is in pursuit.

Clocked as the fastest of all monkeys or apes, patas monkeys can reach a ground speed of 33 miles (53 kilometers) per hour in three seconds! They bound off in rapid sideways leaps, pursued by troop mates. The game is afoot! To outsmart and outdistance the chaser, the lead patas springs off a sapling, using it like a slingshot to catapult even faster through the air. *Boi-i-i-ng! Whoosh!* This springboarding teaches the art of evasive getaways from hungry cheetahs.

Patas may be the fastest monkeys on land, but Lowe's guenon monkeys are the fastest arboreal acrobats of the West African forest canopy. Games of treetop tag are a favorite activity. *Wheee!* Monkey-bar heaven. These monkeys can easily outdistance a prowling leopard.

### Hide-and-Seek

Mongooses, found mostly in Africa and Asia, and tamarins, found in South America, are both expert hiders. They'll scamper away from playmates or siblings to hide in hollow logs, burrows, or rock crevices. Games of hide-and-seek may prepare these small mammals for quick and sometimes narrow escapes from predators.

# GAMES OF STRENGTH

### King of the Hill

Birds called Arabian babblers lift up a stick, give a play bow, or roll over to invite a fellow babbler to join in a game of King of the Hill. In this test of strength, it's a quick rush at each other to see who can knock the other one sideways off their perch, or "throne." While these games are innocent when the birds are young, they may later serve as a way of determining pecking order or territorial dominance within the group.

### Tug-of-War

Wolf pups from around the world play tug-of-war using sticks, bones, or the skins of dead animals. They will use any of these same objects as a hunting "toy." They will toss it, stalk it, fetch it, then proudly parade it around as though it is a freshly killed animal.

Spotted hyenas, found mostly in Africa, will grab hold of a piece of animal hide or an old wildebeest tail and go at it, letting out whoops, groans, giggles, or *grrrs* as they play. Tug-of-war games strengthen a hyena's jaw muscles and sharpen its reaction time.

Neotropic cormorants, found in South and Central America, enjoy playing fetch with sticks. They also love tug-of-war. Grabbing opposite ends of a stick, a strand of seaweed, or even a fish, a pair of cormorants goes one-on-one in this back-and-forth test of strength.

## Smackdown!

Friendly wrestling is a way to test strength, let off steam, and have a blast. In turns, African lion cubs bite and hold each other in a kind of wrestler's headlock. Play wrestling is good preparation for future fights with hyenas, jackals, or lions from other prides. The strength and moves developed in wrestling are a must for defending territory or taking down prey.

Within a week of being born, meerkat pups, from southern Africa, engage in play fights. They tussle and tumble, chewing on ears, noses, and limbs. Standing on hind legs, they push and shove until one meerkat topples over. *Pur-r-r! Chur-r-r!* The victor jumps on its playmate's tummy. Smackdown! Besides fostering bonding, this play readies the meerkats physically and mentally should another group of meerkats make a move to take over their territory.

# GAMES OF DEXTERITY

### Beware the Venom!

Meerkats love to eat scorpions. But a scorpion's sting can be deadly. To teach young pups how to outsmart this venomous arachnid, older, more experienced meerkats provide the pups with a dead scorpion to bat around. After a few trial runs with a dead scorpion, they graduate to stalking a live scorpion whose stinger has been removed. If the scorpion manages to get away, the older meerkat brings it back. *Crunch!* The game does not usually end well for the scorpion.

### Pat-a-Cake, Pat-a-Cake

Clapping games such as pat-a-cake can be seen and heard on any playground. These games help with hand-eye coordination and dexterity. But humans aren't the only ones to engage in hand-clapping and slapping games. Joeys, or young kangaroos, get up on their hind legs to slap and clap with their moms, playing a boxing game that looks like the familiar "Pat-a-cake, pat-a-cake, baker's man." Using open paws and a flat-footed stance, the moms are careful not to hurt the joeys. Animal researchers call the mothers' carefulness "self-handicapping."

Hares and rabbits can also be seen standing on their hind legs while batting and patting at one another with their forepaws.

## Rock Play

Young Japanese macaques, or snow monkeys, roll, shape, and play with snowballs. Older snow monkeys play similarly with rocks. This recent discovery by professor Michael Huffman is called "stone handling." Huffman notes that some monkeys roll the rocks, while others click them together or hoard them. Not to be left out, younger monkeys gather stones as well. Like human children playing with blocks, they stack the rocks and take pleasure in knocking over the pile. They even keep a favorite stone to cuddle and hold. Pet rock, anyone? Researchers have found that the stone-handling monkeys live longer and continue to have better brain function and memory than their less dexterous relatives.

Move over, Bozo the Clown. There's a new juggler in town! Lying on their back on a riverbank, North American river otters roll and slide as many as three rocks at a time across their chest, down their arms, and even along their face. They toss rocks onto their face, up over their nose, and back around again. They often have a favorite rock or two that they carry around all their lives in hidden pockets under their arms. One theory suggests that rock juggling may help with dexterity needed to wrest meat from clams and mussels.

# PUZZLES AND BRAIN GAMES

## Operation

If you've ever played the game Operation, you know it requires good hand-eye coordination, as well as fine motor skills. The cactus finch of the Galápagos Islands plays a similar game. It starts by finding a grub. Instead of eating the little wiggler, the finch pushes the grub into a crack or crevice of a tree. In place of the tweezers used in Operation, the bird deftly uses a spine of cactus to poke, prod, and pry loose the grub from its hiding place. Practice makes perfect!

## Treasure Hunt

Ravens are mischievous birds, and they love to play a kind of treasure hunt game. It begins when one raven flies off to hide a stick, stone, or found object. If another raven senses what's going on, it will start searching for whatever that other raven might have hidden away. Researchers believe that the game works to refine the ravens' hiding skills. The better hidden their caches of food are, the less likely they are to be found and stolen by other birds.

# PART II
# JUST FOR KICKS

# HANGING AROUND

### Play Clothes

Like many primates, juvenile orangutans are agile treetop tumblers, swinging and swaying up in the canopy. Young orangutans will also play dress-up, draping themselves with costumes made of leaves, vines, branches, twigs, or other vegetation.

# GAMES FOR BONDING

### Pop Goes the Wallaby!

While safely tucked inside Mom's pouch, baby wallabies entertain themselves with a bouncy game of "Now you see me, now you don't."

### Peekaboo

A common chimpanzee mother plays peekaboo with her babies. A mother chimp might hide behind a tree, then pop back out with glee, to the utter delight of her child.

### Tummy Time!

Bonobos, close relatives of chimps, are also playful. A human baby's first airplane ride is often a pretend one, flying through the air balanced on a parent's feet. Bonobos like to give their babies airplane rides, too. The mini test flights prepare a baby for swinging and soaring through the forest canopy. *Whee!* Touch the sky! Even as adults, bonobos chase, nibble, tickle, and laugh for hours.

### Giddy-up!

High in the mountains of eastern Central Africa lives the impressive mountain gorilla. Gorilla mothers, like chimp mothers, tickle, swing, and hug their offspring. Gorilla dads make great playmates, too, giving youngsters in the family bouncy rides on their back. These silverbacks—so called for the silver stripe down the center of their back—get a Best Dad Award.

# CATCH!

## Drop and Dive

Seagulls are known to carry a clam into the sky, then drop it onto a hard surface, such as a rock or paved road. The clam cracks open and the gull swoops down to eat a tasty meal. When they're not hungry, herring, black-backed, common, and Pacific gulls drop clams over a soft surface like dirt, grass, or sand, so that if it does hit ground, it won't break. After releasing the clam, the gull dives after it, trying to catch it before it hits the ground. Researchers note that gulls play the game more often when the wind is strong, providing a greater challenge.

Sea lions and seals play the same game in the water with starfish or puffer fish they've dislodged from rocks or crevices, allowing them to free-fall for a while before going in for the interception!

## Fetch!

Nicknamed "flying footballs" for their stout body shape, green herons sometimes toss a stick, leaf, rootlet, seedpod, or other plant debris to the ground, just so they can go retrieve the object and do it all over again. In the water, they do the same with a fish, dead or alive.

A Lowe's guenon monkey grabs a twig, branch, or stone and races with it up into the treetops. From its high perch, the monkey drops the object and just watches it fall. *Crack! Bang!* resounds through the forest as the object ricochets off branches on its way down. The instant the object hits the ground, the guenon monkey scurries back down the tree to fetch it. Back up the tree it scampers to drop and fetch again. Isn't gravity great?

# CLOWNING AROUND

### Pranksters

Keas, a type of bird in the parrot family from the Southern Alps of New Zealand, are among the most impish of all birds. These "clowns of the mountains" actually steal glasses, pens, keys, or even money from people. They've even been known to snatch a child's pacifier! Sometimes keas prank each other, sneaking up to yank a leg or to grab a beak. If a kea rolls on its back, this cues another kea to jump up and down on its playmate's tummy. *Boing! Boing!* It's a tummy trampoline!

### When Push Comes to Shove

While on land, beaver kits get into brief upright shoving matches. To the human eye, they can look a little like sumo wrestlers. It's a friendly process of getting to know each other.

### Elephant Bowling

African elephant calves often change the group they play with, making buddies from other elephant families. They push, roll, and jostle, play-slapping each other with their trunks. Should a calf get knocked down, its mother or another female steps in to help it back up with her powerful trunk.

A researcher once witnessed a herd of African elephants meandering along a river. Up on the embankment, a young male squatted out of sight, as if lying in wait. When one of the older elephants down at the river's edge began to trundle up the slope, the young male slid down, aimed directly at the climbing elephant, and bowled it over. The two tumbled to the bottom, where they playfully trunk-wrestled. Just as they were starting to make their way back up the muddy slope—*Ba-r-r-o-o-o*, trumpeted another elephant up on the embankment. Down it came, sliding. *Bam!* A perfect strike!

# THRILL SEEKERS

### I Feel Dizzy

For unknown reasons, bonobos and some other great apes like to run around with their eyes closed. Field primatologists theorize that these playful runs may be for the new, the unexpected, or just the adrenaline rush of an unpredictable situation. *Thwap!* Watch out for vines, tree trunks, and low-hanging branches . . . not to mention crouching lions.

Rainbow lorikeets, found in Australia, as well as parrots and crows from North and South America, enjoy hanging upside down and swinging from tree branches and vines. Head rush! They chatter and call out in wild excitement all the while.

# DASHING THROUGH THE SNOW

### Sledding

Polar bears, from the Far North, and penguins, from Antarctica, love to slide down snowy hills or chutes and climb right back up to do it again. Each animal has its own style of sliding, whether face-first and stomach down, or feetfirst, gliding on its back.

Like polar bears, ravens and crows across the United States and Canada enjoy a fast slide on their bellies or a rolling tumble down a pile of snow. These birds have even learned to fashion makeshift sleds out of found objects such as lids from cans to speed down snow-covered rooftops.

River otters, when not playing with or juggling their favorite rocks, slide down banks of mud or snow, sometimes gliding right over each other in their enthusiasm and squeaking with joy.

# IN THE WATER

### Surf's Up!

At Cable Beach in Broome, Western Australia—and at many beaches along the northern coast of Australia—giant saltwater crocodiles have been observed body-surfing in the swelling waves. It's plenty fun for the croc, but watch out, surfers! It's not just great white sharks that might be hungry.

Hummingbirds love to jump into and ride any stream of rushing water, even the spray of a garden hose held by a human. *Whoosh!*

### Marco? Polo!

What would summer be without pool games? Rhesus monkeys, whose home range extends from Afghanistan to eastern China, love diving and splashing in the water, which might include playing pranks on one another. These mischievous monkeys particularly relish catching others off guard by swimming under them and yanking a leg to pull them under.

Hyenas, too, like to swim and play as a pack in the water, chasing one another in and out of the pool, splashing, dunking, and yapping all the while.

## Blowing Bubbles

While frolicking, a dolphin blows large ring-shaped bubbles, then chases them, pokes them, and pushes its nose through the bubble rings, over and over, like playing with a toy. A Hula-Hoop for the snout!

## Water Dancing

Renowned primatologist Jane Goodall has observed that chimpanzees (mostly males), when they come upon a waterfall, swing, sway, and perform what she calls "dancing" to the rhythm of the rushing water. Overcome with what seems to be awe, the chimps can be seen wading into the water. They toss rocks or logs into the stream, then twirl around or grab hold of a low hanging vine and swing-spin out over the tumbling spray.

# GLOSSARY

**acrobat:** one that performs gymnastic feats requiring skillful control of the body

**adrenaline:** a hormone released into the body's circulatory system, especially when under stress; increases blood flow and breathing rate and allows muscles to work more efficiently during physical exertion

**agility:** the ability to move quickly and easily

**apex predator:** also called *top predator* or *top carnivore*; any flesh-eating animal at the top of the food chain that is not preyed on by any other animal; *see also* predator

**arachnid:** a class of wingless eight-legged animals that includes spiders, ticks, mites, and scorpions

**arboreal:** living in trees

**cache:** a collection of items stored in a hidden or inaccessible place

**capacity:** the maximum amount that something can contain

**crevice:** a narrow opening or fissure, especially in a rock or wall

**debris:** scattered pieces of waste or remains

**dexterity:** skill in performing tasks, especially with the hands

**fine motor skills:** the movements and coordination of the small muscles of a body, often thought of as movements that involve the fingers and hands

**formidable:** inspiring fear or respect through being impressively large, powerful, intense, or capable

**gravity:** an invisible force that pulls objects with mass toward each other

**gyration:** a rapid movement in a circle or spiral; a whirling motion

**hand-eye coordination:** the way that hands and sight work together in order to do things that require speed and accuracy (such as catching or hitting a ball)

**headlock:** a method of restraining another by holding an arm firmly around the head, especially as a hold in wrestling

**hormones:** regulatory substances produced in an organism and transported in tissue fluids such as blood or sap to stimulate specific cells or tissues into action

**interception:** the action or fact of preventing someone or something from continuing to a destination

**juke:** to fake out in sports by making a sham move to mislead an opponent

**predator:** an organism that kills and eats other organisms

**pride:** a group of lions living together as a family unit; a lion pride may include up to three males, a dozen females, and their young

**primatologist:** a scientist who studies primates, an order of mammals that includes apes, monkeys, and lemurs

**stalk:** to hunt for prey by following it in a stealthy manner

**territory:** the area that a species of animal consistently defends against intruders

**theory:** a carefully thought-out explanation for observations of the natural world that brings together facts, ideas, and guesses

# BIBLIOGRAPHY

## Books

Ackerman, Jennifer. *The Bird Way: A New Look at How Birds Talk, Work, Play, Parent, and Think*. New York: Penguin, 2020.

Bateson, Patrick, and Paul Martin. *Play, Playfulness, Creativity and Innovation*. New York: Cambridge University Press, 2013.

Bekoff, Marc. *The Emotional Lives of Animals: A Leading Scientist Explores Animal Joy, Sorrow, and Empathy—and Why They Matter*. Novato, CA: New World Library, 2007.

Bekoff, Marc, and John A. Byers, eds. *Animal Play: Evolutionary, Comparative, and Ecological Perspectives*. Cambridge, UK: Cambridge University Press, 1998.

Burghardt, Gordon M. *The Genesis of Animal Play: Testing the Limits*. Cambridge, MA: MIT Press, 2006.

Fagen, Robert. *Animal Play Behavior*. New York: Oxford University Press, 1981.

O'Connell, Caitlin. *Wild Rituals: 10 Lessons Animals Can Teach Us About Connection, Community and Ourselves*. San Francisco: Chronicle Prism, 2021.

Recio, Belinda. *Inside Animal Hearts and Minds: Bears That Count, Goats That Surf, and Other True Stories of Animal Intelligence and Emotion*. New York: Skyhorse, 2017.

Toomey, David. *Kingdom of Play: What Ball-bouncing Octopuses, Belly-flopping Monkeys, and Mud-slinging Elephants Reveal about Life Itself*. New York: Scribner, 2024.

## Articles

Cougar, Bridget. "Wild Animals at Play." *Medium*, May 22, 2020. https://medium.com/illumination/wild-animals-at-play-982e26ea57f0.

O'Connell, Caitlin. "Play Is Serious Business for Elephants." *Scientific American*, August 1, 2021. https://www.scientificamerican.com/article/play-is-serious-business-for-elephants/.

Pozis-Francois, Orit, Amotz Zahavi, and Avishag Zahavi. "Social Play in Arabian Babblers." *Behaviour* 141, no. 4 (April 2004): 425–450. https://www.jstor.org/stable/4536139?seq=1.

Vance, Erik. "Where the Wild Things Play." *New York Times*, July 21, 2020. https://www.nytimes.com/2020/07/21/parenting/animal-behavior-play-games.html.

## Videos

ABC Melbourne. "White Kangaroo Joey Plays Hide-and-Seek from Mum's Pouch." Facebook video, May 25, 2020. https://www.facebook.com/watch/?v=271619367360346.

Bisi, Mark. "Otter Juggling Rocks: A Few Theories Why." The Dodo. YouTube video, March 1, 2017. https://www.youtube.com/watch?v=U7bvq0VEnYA.

Newsflare. "Sea Lion Plays with Puffer Fish Like a Ball." Dailymotion video, 2017. https://www.dailymotion.com/video/x5jabyf.

# ACKNOWLEDGMENTS

The author wishes to extend special thanks to Regina Villarreal for her astute eye and structural acumen; to Eliza Edwards, reader extraordinaire; and to Mary Lee Donovan, an insightful and encouraging voice.

# INDEX

To Megan, my Polaris, my North Star
RH

For Kiera—thank you for reminding me
how important it is for even grown-ups to play!
SL

Epigraph from *The Descent of Man* by Charles Darwin, 1871

First edition 2025

Library of Congress Catalog Card Number pending
ISBN 978-1-5362-3090-1

25 26 27 28 29 30 CCP 10 9 8 7 6 5 4 3 2 1

Printed in Shenzhen, Guangdong, China

This book was typeset in PT Sans.
The illustrations were created digitally.

Candlewick Press
99 Dover Street
Somerville, Massachusetts 02144

www.candlewick.com

EU Authorized Representative: HackettFlynn Ltd., 36 Cloch Choirneal,
Balrothery, Co. Dublin, K32 C942, Ireland. EU@walkerpublishinggroup.com